It's Possible!

It's Possible!

— A JOURNAL FOR LEADERS AND OTHER KIDS OF ALL AGES —

Heidi Boerstler

Copyright © 2015 Heidi Boerstler
All rights reserved

ISBN-13: 9781507765326
ISBN-10: 1507765320

Also by Heidi Boerstler

Soaring! New Thinking on Leadership
Soaring Act Two: Leading into Leadership
The Workbook of Transformational Leadership
Your Tool Chest for Animating Leadership

What should I be but just what I am?

—Edna Saint Vincent Millay

For Miriam
Always sweetness

Introduction

Today is your day!
Your mountain is waiting, so…get on your way!

—Dr. Seuss, *Oh the Places You'll Go*

It's Possible! A Journal for Leaders and Other Kids of All Ages grew out of my work with leaders and future leaders in every kind of organization. They asked for a way to recognize and connect with their unique gifts and talents in order to create new beginnings for themselves and for their organizations and everyone in them.

Creativity always begins with a seed. Your seed is already within you, waiting for encouragement so it can grow.

My intent in creating this journal is to help you connect with the creativity you knew as a child. All you need is an open heart and a willingness to risk searching in places other people are not able or willing to go.

There has never been anyone else quite like you, and there never will be.

You are here to make life better for having lived it.

—Heidi Boerstler

Piglet: How do you spell love?
Pooh: You don't spell it. You feel it.

—A. A. Milne, *Winnie-the-Pooh*

Describe three things that immediately bring a smile to your face.

There are far, far better things ahead than any we leave behind.

—C. S. Lewis, twentieth-century British author

Describe one of your dreams that hasn't come true yet (a new job or role, an activity, a relationship, or something else).

Many things are possible just as long as you don't know they're impossible.

—Norton Juster, *The Phantom Tollbooth*

It has been said that you never know what you have until you lose it. Think of something you lost recently (a relationship, a possession, a job, or something else). What have you gained from the experience?

*When there's a smile in your heart,
There's no better time to start.*

J.M. Barrie, Peter Pan

Describe places you plan to visit. You can go anywhere you'd like (to a new geographic location or any other place you haven't visited before).

Just because an animal is large, it doesn't mean
He doesn't want kindness; however big Tigger seems to be,
Remember that he wants kindness as much as Roo.

A.A. Milne, Winnie-the-Pooh

Describe one thing you recently chose to do for someone. How did it make you feel? What was the other person's reaction?

*It's not much of a tail,
But I'm sort of attached to it.*

A.A. Milne, Winnie-the-Pooh

If you could own only four possessions for the rest of your life, what would they be?
 Draw them here.

I am not afraid of storms, for I am learning how to sail my ship.

—Louisa May Alcott, *Little Women*

Focus on something in your life that is currently causing you difficulty. Describe how you might keep sailing despite the storms.

Keep adventuring and stay not a grown up.

J.M. Barrie, Peter Pan

Focus on beginning something new today (exploring a new place, having a new conversation, or doing something else). Describe your experience.

> *Inside all of us is HOPE*
> *Inside all of us is FEAR*
> *Inside all of us is ADVENTURE*
> *Inside all of us is…A WILD THING*
>
> —Maurice Sendak, *Where the Wild Things Are*

Write down your favorite, most daring dream on a piece of paper.

Fold it up and hold it in your hand.

Toss it into the air. It is now part of creation.

"Sometimes," said Pooh, "the tiniest things take up the most room in your heart."

—A. A. Milne, *Winnie-the-Pooh*

Everyone has experienced miracles in life, such as a beautiful sunrise, the birth of a child, or a garden growing. What is your experience with miracles? When do you recognize the miraculous?

The greatest secrets are hidden in the most unlikely places.

—Roald Dahl, *Charlie and the Chocolate Factory*

Circle the things in your life you pay the most attention to.

clothes   shoes   travel   money   love   success   beauty

fame   social media   family   entertainment   possessions   power

your home   your pets   your partner   God   heavenly spirits

music   art   shopping   religion   health   fitness   exercise

gratitude   forgiveness   celebration   prayer   other

Now underline the things you'd rather focus your attention on.

It's no use to go back to yesterday because I was a different person then.

—Lewis Carroll, *Alice's Adventures in Wonderland*

What in your life is well traveled (repetitive thoughts or behaviors, boxes of old possessions stored for years, and so forth)? What part of you is living in the past?

Anything's possible if you've got enough nerve.

—J. K. Rowling, *Harry Potter and the Philosopher's Stone*

Fill these circles with three of your biggest fears; then color them in until you can't see the fear anymore.

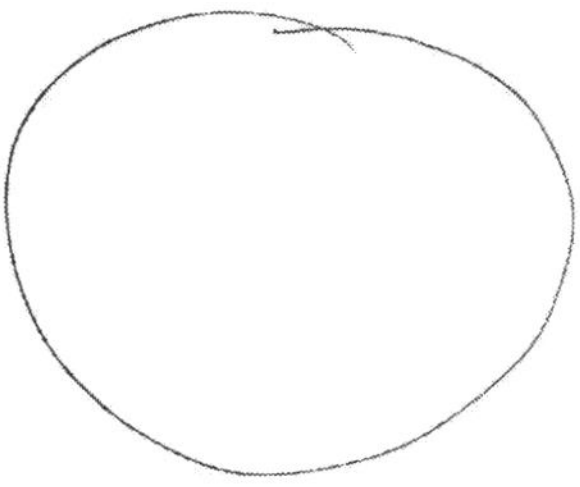

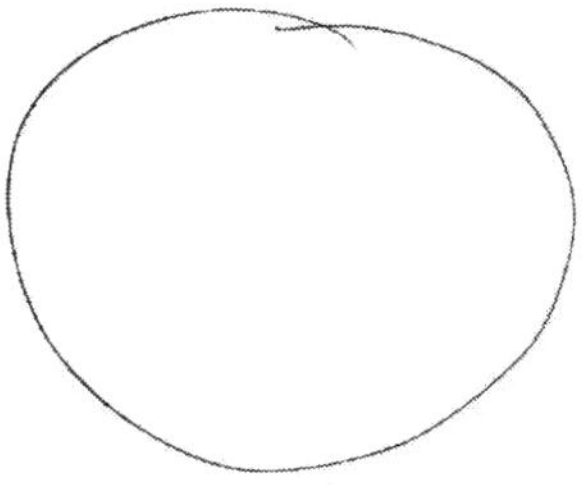

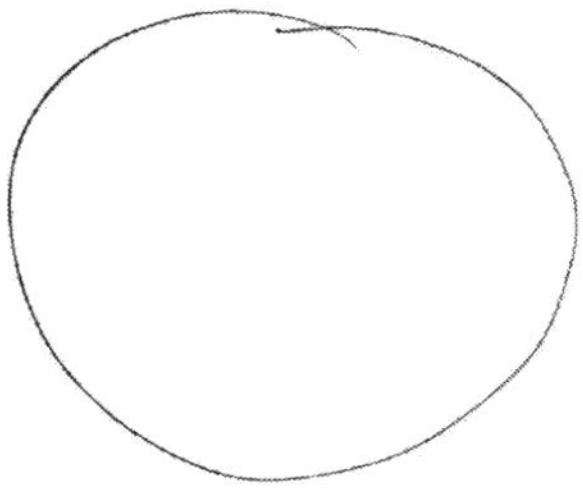

You have brains in your head. You have feet in your shoes.
You can steer yourself any direction you choose. You're on your own.
And you know what you know. And you are the one who'll decide where to go.

—Dr. Seuss, *Oh, the Places You'll Go!*

Focus on a significant relationship that you are struggling with (a work relationship, a personal relationship, or something else). Describe the choices you might make and how this relationship can be rejuvenated.

Isn't it nice to think that tomorrow is a new day with no mistakes in it yet?

—L. M. Montgomery, *Anne of Green Gables*

When do you choose to risk?

When do you play it safe?

You know how you let yourself think, that everything will be all right if you can only get to a certain place or do a certain thing. But when you get there you find it's not that simple.

—Richard Adams, *Watership Down*

Describe something in your life you would like to leave behind.

If things start happening, don't worry, don't stew. Just go right along and you'll start happening too.

—Dr. Seuss, *Oh, the Places You'll Go!*

Sometimes, because of our age or for other reasons, we might think it's too late to chase a new possibility.
Why it's never too late to chase a possibility.

True courage is facing danger when you're afraid.

—Frank Baum, *The Wonderful Wizard of Oz*

Describe a time when you kept moving forward even though you were afraid.

Happiness can be found even in the darkest of times if only one remembers to turn on the light.

—J. K. Rowling, *Harry Potter and the Philosopher's Stone*

Focus on a difficult experience you had in your life. Describe one thing you have learned from the experience.

How sweet to be a cloud
Floating in the Blue!
Every little cloud
Always sings aloud.

—A. A. Milne, *Winnie-the-Pooh*

Go outside and watch the clouds as they move across the sky. Draw the clouds here.

What do they teach you?

A person's a person no matter how small.

—Dr. Seuss, *Horton Hears a Who!*

Values I want to live by: Why I want to live by them:

The moment when you doubt whether you can fly, you cease forever being able to do it.

—J. M. Barrie, *Peter Pan*

What possibilities are you open to?

For what you see and hear depends a good deal on where you are standing: it also depends on what sort of person you are.

—C. S. Lewis, *The Magician's Nephew*

Name three ideas you fundamentally disagree with, ideas that are harmful to your spirit and your well-being (for example, assumptions about certain groups of people).

Write them down on three sheets of paper. Now tear them up.

If there ever is tomorrow when we're not together…there is something you must remember. You are braver than you believe, stronger than you seem, and smarter than you think. .

—A. A. Milne, *The House at Pooh Corner*

When you find an exciting new possibility, what keeps you from chasing it?

Second star to the right and straight on 'til morning

J.M. Barrie, Peter Pan

Sit quietly.

What is calling to you in your life?

Don't try to comprehend with your mind. Your minds are very limited. Use your intuition.

—Madeleine L'Engle, *A Wrinkle in Time*

Think of an issue you've been approaching by thinking logically. How might you consider this issue through your heart instead?

No one has ever become poor by giving.

—Anne Frank, *The Diary of Anne Frank*

Focus on something you recently gave away. Draw it here.

I'm a great believer in luck, and I find the harder I work, the more I have of it.

—Thomas Jefferson, third president of the United States

Something I think I need luck for: How I can get it without luck:

You have been my friend. That in itself is a tremendous thing.

—E. B. White, *Charlotte's Web*

List your sources of the following:

Happiness

Love

Courage

Friendship

Strength

Laughter

Weeds are flowers too, once you get to know them.

A.A. Milne, Winnie-the-Pooh

Describe something about yourself that pushes people away.

Now describe how that same thing connects you.

Some people care too much. I think it's called love.

A.A. Milne, Winnie-the-Pooh

Color in all the emotions you've experienced.

anger   hurt   jealousy   joy   stress   frustration   empathy

pride   tension   envy   embarrassment   hope   disgust

irritation   guilt   shame   love   courage

Are there any blank areas?

The only person you are destined to become is the person you decide to be.

—Ralph Waldo Emerson, nineteenth-century American author

List three traits you'd like others to see in you.

Think left and think right, think low and think high, Oh the Thinks you can think up
if only you try.

—Dr. Seuss, *Oh, the Thinks You Can Think!*

Name your three most frequent thoughts (thoughts about work, family, or something else).

What would you rather think about?

We all have magic inside us.

—J. K. Rowling, *Harry Potter and the Sorcerer's Stone*

In each circle, write the things that matter for each area of your life.

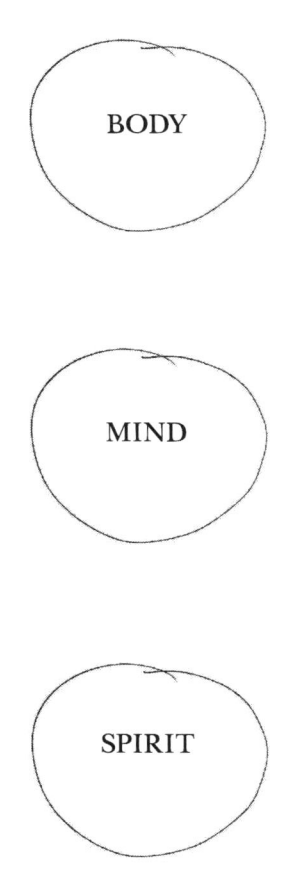

BODY

MIND

SPIRIT

No act of kindness, no matter how small, is ever wasted.

—Aesop, *The Lion and the Mouse*

Fill these hearts by writing in acts of kindness.

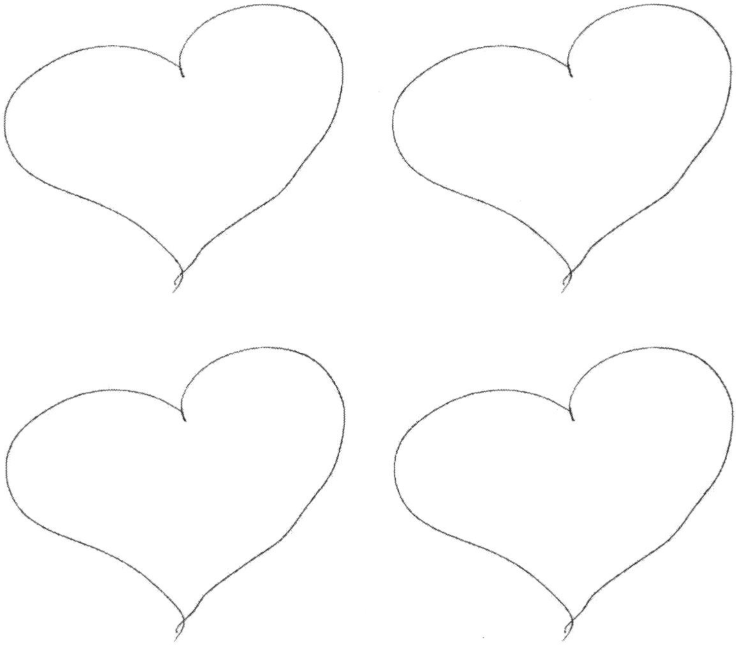

I am not afraid. I was born to do this.

—Joan of Arc, fifteenth-century French revolutionary and Roman Catholic saint

What is your greatest motivation in life?

Say it out loud. Make it a part of each breath.

Now move forward.

Sometimes I've believed as many as six impossible things before breakfast.

—Lewis Carroll, *Through the Looking Glass*

Focus on your ideal life, the one that makes your heart leap. Write it on your star.

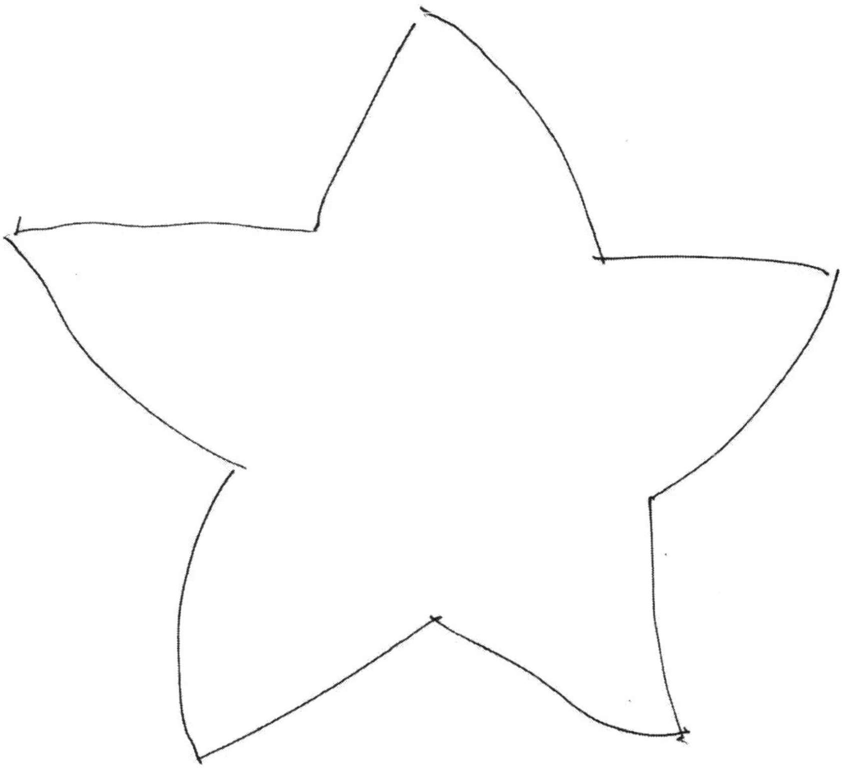

When something happens in your life that rattles you, come back to this page and remember what you most want in your life. How are your choices moving you toward your star?

To live will be an awfully big adventure.

J.M. Barrie, Peter Pan

Fill in each circle with the people, activities, and feelings you have room for.

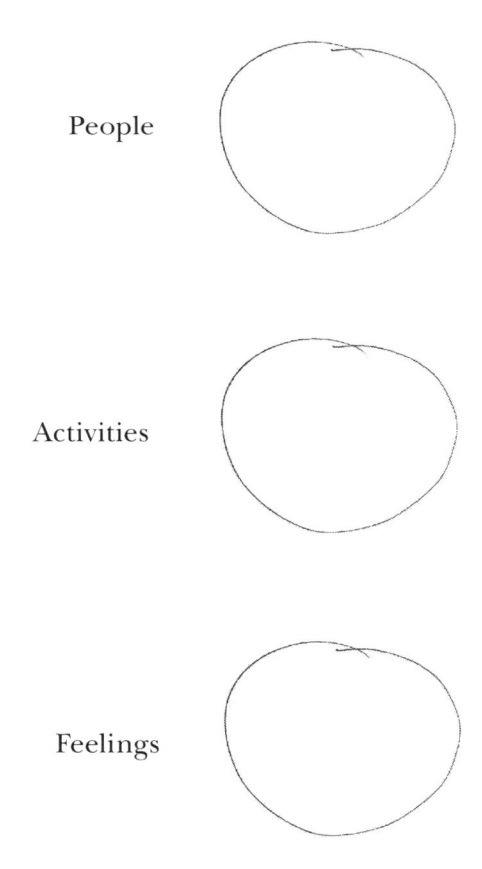

People

Activities

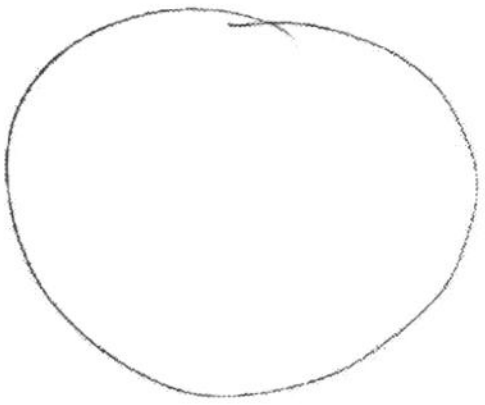

Feelings

Be yourself. Everyone else is already taken.

—Oscar Wilde, Irish playwright

Draw a portrait of yourself using the colors and patterns that reflect who you are.

All of the magic I have known, I've had to make myself.

—Anonymous

Write about something you have made out of nothing. It can be anything, such as a friendship, a poem, or a new perspective.

*Shall we make a new rule of life from tonight:
always try to be a little kinder than necessary.*

J.M. Barrie, Peter Pan

Strength is found in the deepest places. Draw the source of your greatest strength here.

Time is not at all what it seems. It does not flow in only one direction, and the future exists simultaneously with the past.

—Albert Einstein, twentieth-century, German-born theoretical physicist

Focus on your place in the universe and the ancestors who are part of your DNA. They are pushing you forward. Think about how the particles you're made of are also the same particles that make up the earth, moon, and stars. Draw your particles here.

I knew who I was in the morning, but I've changed a few times since then.

—Lewis Carroll, *Alice's Adventures in Wonderland*

Think of a major transformation you've been through in your life (a new perspective, career, course of study, relationship, or something else). What is one lesson you learned?

Reality leaves a lot to the imagination.

—Anonymous

Mark where you fall on the following spectrums:

Kind   Unkind

Patient   Impatient

Open   Closed

Giving   Receiving

Listener   Talker

Now mark where you would like to fall.

I knew when I met you an adventure was going to happen.

A.A. Milne, Winnie-the-Pooh

Think about all the people whose lives you affect. Draw them here.

*Piglet noticed that even though he had a very small heart,
It could hold a rather large amount of gratitude.*

A.A. Milne, Winnie-the-Pooh

List three aspects of your life that you are grateful for.

Somewhere, something incredible is waiting to be known.

—Carl Sagan, twentieth-century American astronomer

Go outside at night, and look into the vastness of the universe. Make a wish and write it down here.

Repeat this exercise once a month until you have a page full of wishes that are out in the world, slowly taking shape.

We can all dance when we find music we love.

—Giles Andreae, *Giraffes Can't Dance*

Think of a problem you are facing. How can you make choices with truth and courage?

One never knows.

—Antoine de Saint-Exupery, French writer and philosopher

This page is not blank.

It is filled with every possibility.

It is your future.

All the world is made of faith and trust and pixie dust.

—J. M. Barrie, *Peter Pan*

Remember yourself as a child. Given what you know now, what advice would you give your young self?

How lucky I am to have something that makes saying good-bye so hard.

—A. A. Milne, *Winnie-the-Pooh*

Focus on the pain that visits you from time to time. Write it down, and then turn the page.

"My dear young fellow," the Old-Green-Grasshopper *said gently.* *"There are a whole lot of things in this world of ours you haven't started wondering about yet."*

—Roald Dahl, *James and the Giant Peach*

Name one part of your life that you wish were different. In what way are you grateful for this part of your life?

Never do anything by halves if you want to get away with it. Be outrageous. Go the whole hog. Make sure everything you do is so completely crazy it's unbelievable.

—Roald Dahl, *Matilda*

Fill in this tree to create your own life map.

Birds don't need ornithologists to fly.

—Mark Nepo, poet and philosopher

Focus on what makes you feel the most alive. Write it down.

You can't pick out the pieces you like and leave the rest. Being part of the whole thing, that's the blessing.

—Natalie Babbitt, *Tuck Everlasting*

About the Author

Heidi Boerstler, Dr.PH, JD, is a professor of transformational leadership, ethics, and law at the Business School, University of Colorado at Denver. Her degrees are from Northwestern University, the University of Denver, and Yale University. She is a leadership consultant to numerous organizations. Dr. Boerstler was one of only a hundred people chosen for the Winslow Centennial Honor Roll for Excellence from the Yale School of Public Health in honor of the school's centennial.

Made in the USA
San Bernardino, CA
27 January 2016